Fran Fisher, MCC

Editors: Ron Rael, Gloria Maxx, Elizabeth Burroughs-Heineman, MJ Schwader
Photos: Royalty Free
Publisher: FJFisher Publishing

ISBN: 978-0-9798754-6-5

Feel free to share brief quotations from this book with attribution to the author as follows: *Calling Forth Greatness, Seven Coaching Wisdoms for Transforming Your Life,* by Fran Fisher, MCC

www.franfishercoach.com

When you are inspired by some great purpose, some extraordinary project, all your thoughts break their bonds: your mind transcends limitations, your consciousness expands in every direction, and you find yourself in a new, great and wonderful world. Dormant forces, faculties, and talents become alive, and you discover yourself to be a greater person by far than you ever dreamed yourself to be.

- Patañjali

Table of Contents

INTRODUCTION

Coaching is the sacred space of Unconditional Love:
where Learning, Growth, and Transformation naturally occur.
~Fran Fisher, MCC

Imagine a world where we are:

- **Asking** questions with sincere interest and curiosity vs. telling others what to do
- **Championing** the wants and desires of others vs. needing to provide our unsolicited ideas, suggestions, or advice
- **Honoring** respect and confidentiality vs. gossiping about others
- **Providing** positive feedback and acknowledgment vs. making judgmental remarks or acting on our judgments
- **Being** a committed listener vs. a distracted listener
- **Expressing** our opinion without attachment and allowing the other person to express theirs without needing to be right
- **Calling forth the greatness** in ourselves and each other; seeing one another as the sacred beings that we are

Yes, these are guiding principles for coaches. *Imagine a world* where these are the guiding principles for how all of us are being in our relationships. What do you want less of, Struggle, Stress, Disappointment, Chaos? What do you want more of, Freedom, Joy, Prosperity, Peace, Vitality?

Whether you are a professional coach or not, each of the Seven Coaching Wisdoms is designed to spark new insights and perspectives for you. I invite you to be open to the possibility that these guiding principles are transferable to everyday life. When you practice these principles, you will tap into your deepest, most innate wisdom. You will call forth your own greatness and the greatness of others around you. *Transformation in the quality of your life will naturally occur.*

Coaching is a spiritual practice. It is an empowering way of being in service to self and others. It is both a skill set and a way of living that challenges you to expand yourself beyond who you believe yourself to be, to living more fully who you are at your essence.

The root of *spirituality* is the word *spirit*—an inner attitude that recognizes essence, and what is truly meaningful. Spirit is a powerful life-giving creative force flowing through everything in the universe. *Coaching* is a way of being in a co-creative partnership with that life force. Coaches facilitate clients in accessing their Essential Self so that they can live with greater meaning and purpose, success and fulfillment.

Coaching is based on a principle of empowerment that was recognized by Galileo hundreds of years ago: *We cannot teach people anything; we can only help them discover it within themselves.*

The coaching paradigm is built on that key assumption as well as a core belief that everyone is fundamentally creative, capable, and resourceful. The International Coach Federation (ICF) www.coachfederation.org says:

"Standing on this foundation, the coach's responsibility is to:

- Discover, clarify, and align with what the client wants to achieve

- Encourage client self-discovery

- Elicit client-generated solutions and strategies
- Hold the client responsible and accountable"

When I discovered coaching in 1991, I fell in love with a career that felt more like a dream lifestyle than a job. I was earning a living simply being *me*! This realization came home to me during the holiday season of 1992. I was invited to a party where the only person I knew was the hostess. Upon my arrival, she pointed out another party guest who was a Ph.D. in Career Counseling, and she warned me that this woman held a war against coaching and coaches. My intention was to avoid her.

I kept my distance from that woman throughout the evening. All of a sudden, I was caught off guard when, there she was, standing in front of me with her cocktail glass held at eye level between us. Reading my name tag, she confronted me: "Hello, Fran. What do you do for a living?"

Without a moment's thought, I blurted, "I be *me* all day long, and I get paid abundantly for that!" She threw her head back, squinted her eyes, shook her head, turned, and walked away. As I drove home that night, I thought, "It's so *true*! Who I am now is what I do, and what I do now is who I am!"

At some point, early in my coaching career, I shifted my orientation from *doing* coaching with clients to *being* a coach as a way of life and living. I don't mean that I started coaching family, friends, and everyone I met. I mean, I started living the principles of the coaching paradigm as though I had tapped into a reservoir of wisdom that was latent within me.

The most challenging part of becoming a masterful coach, though, was letting go of my attachment to being the expert. Throughout my school years, I held a 4.0-grade average and graduated as valedictorian of my high school class. I didn't fit in the social circle of girls who got invited on dates and school proms. The only attention I got from boys was when they wanted help with their math, chemistry, or history during study hall. So, I ate up that attention. When I was an apartment manager many years later, residents would come into my office to pay the rent. They would sit down and talk with me for hours. I wore mother, sister, friend, counselor, and advisor hats in those conversations. I relished sharing my advice, ideas, stories, and personal wisdom.

Years later, as a student of coaching, I learned to honor the coaching paradigm by holding my clients as the expert of their lives and work, and myself as the expert in the coaching process—forming a partnership with two experts. I began noticing the "high" I would feel on seeing my clients build on their strengths, take greater risks and leaps of faith, and make heroic changes in their lives. That's when I realized that being the expert had been feeding my ego. Now, I am feeding my soul, as I hold my clients as the experts of their lives. I am being the facilitator of calling forth their natural wisdom. And that's, well, *beyond* delicious. It is extraordinarily nourishing, rewarding and fulfilling.

Fran Fisher, MCC
February 2017

- As you read how coaches apply these guiding principles, reflect on how you can implement these principles in your life or work.
- Visualize how your life and the lives of others around you could be empowered.Danci
- Choose an option for your application practice:
    - Pick one Coaching Wisdom as your focus for the DAY or WEEK; notice the impact; notice what you learn
    - Work with a support buddy; share your challenges, progress, and learning; celebrate your results!
- Reflect on the Inquiry provided for a DAY or WEEK
- Design your own Inquiries
- Journal your learning on the pages provided
- Send an email to Fran, sharing your story of your learning, growth, or transformation. fran@franfishercoach.com
- Visit the CallingForthGreatnessBOOK Fan Page to share your stories, ask questions, and support others on their journey: www.facebook.com/fran.fisher.mcc

Wisdom ONE Connect Heart-to-Heart

I have little doubt that the heart is the major energy center of my body and a conveyor of a code that represents my Soul.
~Paul Pearsall, PhD

It is the time to start appreciating the power of the heart and begin to recognize it as the true wisdom center of our mind-body-spirit humanity.

Coaches establish trust and rapport with clients by showing genuine care and concern for their client's welfare. They create a safe, supportive environment by demonstrating personal integrity, honesty, and respect for client's perceptions, learning style, and personal being. When I center myself in this heart-based mindset, I find it easier to suspend my judgments, which is critical for sustaining a safe environment for my clients to "do their personal work."

According to scientific research and personal experiences, Paul Pearsall, Ph.D., psychoneuroimmunologist, demonstrates in his book *The Heart's Code*, page 4, that the human heart, not the brain, holds the secrets that link body, mind, and spirit. "...Research suggests that the heart thinks, cells remember, and that both of these processes are related to an as yet mysterious, incredibly powerful, but very subtle energy with properties unlike any other known force. This heart's code is recorded and remembered in every cell in the body as an informational template of the soul, always resonating within and from us, sent forth from our heart."

Coaches will:

- **Establish a connection of safety, trust, and caring.**
    - Connecting heart-to-heart is not just something they do. It is how they are being. Coaches center and connect with their heart; bring their awareness to the present moment and to the presence of the heart of the other person; allow themselves to be receptive and open; clear their mind of limiting thoughts, beliefs, or concerns; suspend their judgments and release their attachments. This creates a sacred space.

- **Focus attention on the other person.**
    - Intend to connect on a heart level. Coaches tune into the energy connection between them and their clients; listen deeply to the other person; demonstrate caring with empathy and compassion; commit to supporting their client's clarity and freedom to make more empowering choices.

- **Listen for what the other person is attracted to.**
    - Coaches listen for the client's values—what they would value if they could have what they want, what lights up their heart, or what their heart desires. Coaches reflect what they see or feel from their client's expressions and then check in for clarification and validation. For example: "I notice your eyes lit up when you spoke about your passion for dancing. Is that what your heart wants?"

When we make caring connections, we build more meaningful personal and business relationships. The power of the heart creates safety, trust, and openness. It clears obstacles, expands possibilities, and supports others close to us in our families and work environments in being at choice and empowers them to move toward what "lights them up."

The key to connecting heart-to-heart is authentically caring. Caring is not just another emotion; it is fundamental to most other emotions. For example, you aren't angry or sad unless you care about something that has been lost or damaged. We care because we have wants and needs. Care also has to do with action. We take care to be accurate; we take care to get the outcomes we want. We take care of others—patients, clients, children, parents, etc. Caring can be the link between our emotions and our actions.

Calling Forth Greatness Inquiry: How do I create caring, heart-to-heart connections?

Reflect on this Calling Forth Greatness Inquiry in your journal for a day or a week. Notice what shows up. Journal your learning here:

____

____

____

Care is a fundamental dimension of all action. It can be present or absent, but in either case it has a fundamental shaping of how the action is carried out, and the meaning and value of the outcomes to be produced.
~Robert Dunham

Wisdom TWO Make Empowering Choices

We stand at the crossroads, each minute, each hour, each day, making choices. We choose the thoughts we allow ourselves to think, the passions we allow ourselves to feel, and the actions we allow ourselves to perform. Each choice is made in the context of whatever value system we've selected to govern our lives. In selecting that value system, we are, in a very real way, making the most important choice we will ever make.

~Benjamin Franklin

Coaches help clients raise their awareness of the impact of their choices.

Having choice is an inherent human freedom. You can choose your attitude, opinion, or political or religious affiliations. You can choose your friends, your employer, your interests, habits, and hobbies. You can make a choice between the red or green grapes at the grocery store.

Who you are is determined by the choices you make, so the quality of your life is directly related to how you make your choices. There is a Choice Zone between you and the circumstances in your life.

Imagine standing in your Choice Zone and viewing your life's circumstances through the lens of your "true-self" (vision, mission, purpose, core values, core strengths, etc.). From here you can make empowering choices. Your outcomes will bring greater well-being, ease, prosperity, harmony, and freedom from fear.

Imagine standing outside your Choice Zone and reacting to circumstances or letting the circumstances choose for you.

According to William Glasser, author of *Choice Theory: A New Psychology of Personal Freedom*: "All behavior is chosen, but we only have direct control over the acting and thinking components. We can only control our feeling and physiology indirectly through how we choose to act and think."

Our beliefs and thoughts drive our behavior, which results in our experience and outcomes. Acting from **"true self,"** behavior tends to be more responsible, accepting, allowing, responsive, collaborative, and trusting. Our experience and outcomes are more energizing, expansive, and **powerFULL**.

Acting from fear-based **"false self,"** our behavior tends to be more reactive, critical, competitive, blaming, and controlling. Our experience feels more diminished, at the effect of the circumstances, energy draining, victimized, and **powerLESS.**

We cannot choose our external circumstances,
but we can always choose how we respond to them.
~Epictetus

What are circumstances in life? The baby is crying. Traffic is gridlocked. You are late for an appointment. Your mother died.

The car broke down on the freeway. Your co-worker is absent today. Your hair is turning gray. Your spouse snores. Your wallet was stolen. Your computer hard drive crashed. Gasoline is expensive. A neighbor's dog barked all night. You may be single and lonely. Hate your job. A spouse leaves the toilet seat up. There was a missed flight connection. The wrong person got elected.

Living from the "inside" means making choices that align with your vision, purpose, core values, and empowering beliefs. It means shifting your perception, changing your attitude, or finding an empowering view that brings you a sense of peace and freedom from pain or stress. Making empowering choices in relationship to the circumstances in your life will support you in being more confident, calm, peaceful, creative, energized, free, satisfied, and more fulfilled.

Empowering choices re-connect you to your essential self. Disempowering choices disconnect you from your essential self. Your empowered choices may take courage, faith, time, and patience, but they will transform the quality of your life.

The circumstances may not change immediately, or ever, in some instances. The reality is we have little or no control over many of the circumstances in life—for example, the weather, changing seasons, the commute traffic, hair turning gray, mother dying, or global warming. Other circumstances might be the result of choices we have made in the past or even in the present moment, for example, late for an appointment, took the wrong turn, someone is upset with you, you are sick because you have not been taking care of your personal well-being for a long time.

Here are some EXAMPLES of the Choice Zone:

- **Instead of being judgmental** about my friend's behavior, I choose to be curious and inquire for better understanding. (honoring my Values of friendship, compassion, caring)

- **Instead of resenting** the weather, I choose to look for ways to make it a great day. (Honoring my Values of gratitude, appreciation, positive attitude)

- **Instead of complaining** about my team's results, I choose to be part of the solution. (Honoring my Values of partnership, contribution, responsibility)

Regardless of the circumstances, you have a choice about who you react to the circumstances. And, those choices make the difference between more negativity, upset, and frustration or more inner peace, joy, harmony, and ease.

Consider honoring this guiding principle in life for yourself, as well as offering others the opportunity to make their own empowering choices.

Calling Forth Greatness Inquiry: How am I responding to this circumstance? What is an empowering choice for me?

Reflect on these inquiries in your journal for a day or a week. Notice what shows up. Journal your learning here:

____

____

____

____

____

____

____

____

____

____

____

Between stimulus and response, there is a space. In that space lies our freedom and power to choose our response. In our response lies our growth and freedom.

~Victor Frankl

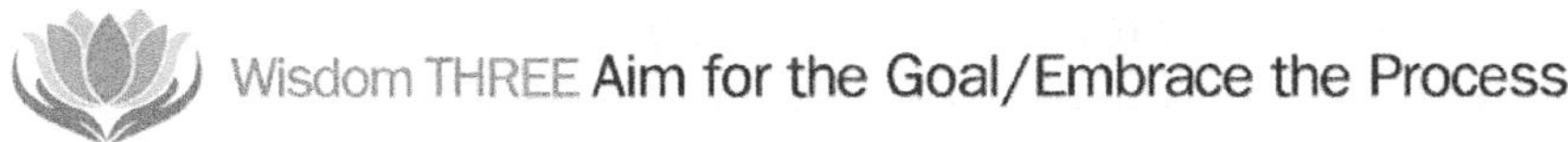

Wisdom THREE Aim for the Goal/Embrace the Process

In the measurement world, we set a goal and strive
to achieve it. In the universe of possibility,
we set the context and let life unfold.
~Benjamin Zander

Coaches recognize there is more energy and aliveness available in the process of moving toward a goal than in the result itself. Clients experience more success, satisfaction, and fulfillment as they embrace the quality of their journey—even with its ups and downs and twists and turns.

The paradox is you can't have a process without setting a goal.

Coaches support clients in embracing these success factors for a quality journey:

- **Be clear** and focused on what you want, and pay no attention to what you don't want.
- **Be committed to achieving the goal.** That sets up creative tension that will pull you forward.
- **Allow head and heart partnership.** Allow each to do what it does best: The heart notices what wants to change, and the head provides the direction and actions for manifesting that desire.
- **Let go of any attachment** to the form of the result, so you don't limit the possibilities.
- **Appreciate your learning and self-discovery.** Hold learning as your value, vs. judging any perceived mistakes, breakdowns, or failures.
- **Be open to the unexpected** (the miracles) along your path. Welcome what shows up, evaluate for learning, and revise your plan based on your self-discovery, step by step. The path *may* be circuitous, but the result will be richer and more satisfying in the end.

You have to accept whatever comes and the only important thing is that you meet it with the best you have to give.
~Eleanor Roosevelt

My client Barry wanted to make a million dollars in his first year of mortgage lending. Suspending my judgment, and *believe me* I had one, in the spirit of partnership, I said, "OK, let's go for it!" In truth, I had no way of knowing what Barry was capable of doing. In the process of going for that goal, Barry could call himself forth powerfully, leverage his natural strengths, learn new skills, and build new practices for success. At the end of that first year, he could blow right by that million and weigh in at 1.5 million or more.

The other possibility was that he could be stopped or slowed down by his limiting beliefs, mental patterns, or emotional blocks. Another possibility is that circumstances beyond his control (global economy, family crisis, natural disaster, etc.) could get in the way or derail him. Thus, his final result could have been less than his goal of a million dollars.

What I knew for sure was that his passion for his goal, his accountability to himself, and his learning process could transform who he is being and who he is becoming in life—beyond mortgage lending.

Calling Forth Greatness Inquiry: Who am I being as I aim for my goal and embrace my process?

Reflect on this Calling Forth Greatness Inquiry in your journal for a day or a week. Notice what shows up. Journal your learning here:

____

____

____

____

____

____

____

____

____

Reach high, for stars lie hidden in your soul.
Dream deep, for every dream precedes the goal.
~Pamela Vault Starr

The road to your dreams
Can only be found
With one foot in eternity
And the other on shaky ground.
~Rick Tourquinio

Wisdom FOUR Speak Empowering Language

Language is power. When we speak,
we exercise the power of language to
transform reality.
~Julia Penelope

A coach uses empowering language and helps clients raise awareness of their language so they can transform their reality.

The words we use express our thoughts, feelings, and attitude. Our thoughts, feelings, and attitude drive our actions. Coaches know that words are clues that identify underlying beliefs and attitudes that may be blocking the client from achieving positive results. Words combined with sound (voice) are energy vibrations that affect us physically, mentally, and emotionally. They have the inherent capacity to give energy or take energy away.

- **Empowering language** is responsible, powerful, and energizing!

- **Disempowering language** is power-less. When we think it, and speak it, we diminish ourselves and others.

Disempowering language keeps us sick and weak.
~Carolyn Myss

Take care to use empowering, energizing, inspiring language when speaking to yourself as well as with others. Negative self-talk can diminish your ability to make positive changes or break through to new levels of success and fulfillment.

What you say and how you say it impacts your experience, whether verbally or in writing. Language has an impact not only on a mental level but also at other subtle levels. Your words can convey underlying messages to your subconscious, evoking physical, emotional, mental, and spiritual implications.

My client Robert was frustrated because he was not making progress toward his goal of finishing his first year in business with a 10% profit. At the same time, he was speaking with language like "I should make more cold calls." When I challenged Robert to make a commitment to an action, he would respond with "probably" or "maybe I will." When he talked about his relationship with his business partner, he would point his finger and use "blame" language, like "He always makes me_____." I offered Robert feedback that his walk and his talk didn't match. In other words, it was like driving his car toward his goal with one foot on the accelerator and one foot on the brake.

Any word or phrase that implies the lack of freedom tends to feel disempowering, such as "have to," "should," "can't," "will not," etc. That language invites a feeling of victimization, which is then reinforced by more disempowering language.

Practice using empowering language such as "I choose to," "I intend to," "I will," "It's important to me," etc. Avoid absolutes, such as "always" and "never." Avoid "I'll try." Instead, it is more powerful to declare what you *will* do.

Speak in "I" language when sharing your experience. Connect with and share your experience vs. speaking in generalities using "you" language. For example, "When I have an insight I feel lighter," vs. "When you have an insight you feel lighter." People listening to your story will be more engaged.

Language is a powerful creative force. You have the opportunity to create what you want more of, beginning with your thoughts. You construct your fortunes and misfortunes with the thoughts you choose to think.

...impulses of energy and information that
we experience as thoughts...are the raw material of the universe.
~Deepak Chopra, MD

Calling Forth Greatness Inquiry: What is my intended impact for what I am thinking or saying?

Reflect on this Calling Forth Greatness Inquiry in your journal for a day or a week. Notice what shows up. Journal your learning here:

____

____

____

____

____

____

Before you speak, ask yourself: Is it kind, is it necessary, is it true, does it improve on the silence?
~Shirdl Sai Baba

Feed a man a fish and he eats for a day.
Teach a man to fish, and he eats for a lifetime.
~Maimonides

The goal of the coaching process is a transformational experience for the client vs. fixing their presenting issue. This is based on the "fishing" principle that Maimonides shared with us thousands of years ago.

Typically, a client will bring an issue to be explored or resolved. Coaches know that the presenting "issue" is rarely the real or underlying "issue." And coaches know that exploring for that deeper issue will provide a greater possibility for a transformation leading to "eating for a lifetime," vs. problem solving at the surface level of "eating for a day."

When we use the term "transformation" in the coaching context, we mean that the client has shifted their relationship to their issue. For example, they are now seeing it from a different perspective, or they have accessed a capacity that frees up their ability to move forward. Most often this shift is from a victim relationship with their issue to an empowered relationship with their issue.

In this context, **transformation = empowerment**: teaching clients to learn how to fish for themselves vs. giving them a fish. The ultimate goal of a coaching conversation is to assist the client in accessing their innate wisdom and building their capacities for resolving their issues going forward.

To illustrate this point, let's say that my executive client, Robert, is having an ongoing problem at work that is causing him lots of stress and impacting his job performance. I ask him to relate his feelings about the situation in a metaphor. He indicates the situation feels like he is on the deck of the Titanic, and he is aware that the ship is sinking. He feels compelled to rearrange the deck chairs, but he keeps getting pulled away to help with the lifeboats.

To explore the metaphor further with him, we imagine I am standing on the deck of that sinking ship with him, and he indicates that rearranging the deck chairs is his immediate priority. If I align with him at this "surface level" of his issue, then together we roll up our sleeves and rearrange the deck chairs to his satisfaction. The chairs are lined up in the number of rows and at the angles he desires. The finished product is aesthetically pleasing for him. We have done a piece of work together and we have accomplished a result. My client is feeling a sense of accomplishment and satisfaction—short-term.

What about long-term?

That's right. There is an underlying issue that has not been addressed. The ship is still going down and we don't know what is driving his need to rearrange those chairs in the circumstances. The underlying issue with his problem at work has not been addressed.

So, committed to supporting my client in shifting his relationship to his problem at work, I invite him to explore underneath his presenting focus. Now my client will have the opportunity to shift his point of view, raising his self-awareness, learning more about himself, and building on capacities that will positively impact all areas of his life—not just the presenting situation.

How do I do that? I will ask Robert, "What's important to you about rearranging the deck chairs?" Let's imagine that he says, "What's important to me is having orderliness." And then I ask, "If you had that orderliness, how would your life be different?" And, he responds, "I would experience freedom from distractions and less stress."

In a real-life coaching conversation, we would now step out of the metaphor and I would invite him to explore how this awareness connects with his current work situation, and what he can learn about himself.

Now we are addressing the deeper "want"—the underlying "issue."

Bless those who challenge us to grow, to stretch, to move beyond the knowable, to come back home to our elemental and essential nature. Bless those who challenge us, for they remind us of doors we have closed and doors we have yet to open.
~Navajo saying

An effective way coaches help clients achieve a deeper, more lasting change is by inviting them to explore the importance, meaning, or motivation for what they want. This opens up access to their essential self and greater self-awareness. Clients begin to feel a sense of freedom to make more empowering choices rather than feeling restricted, stuck, powerless, or a victim of their circumstances.

The deepest "wants" that my clients reveal to themselves are often core values, such as organization, in Robert's case, or integrity, partnership, freedom, clarity, inner peace, well-being, harmony, fairness, trust, etc. From this level of awareness, we will explore how to honor those values more fully. The opportunity from this point is for the client to empower themselves forward.

Do you know that you are a more efficacious voice for transformation in the world than any book, teaching, philosophy or religion? In fact, you are the only dynamic point of transformation that exists!
~Paul Tuttle

Being a catalyst for transformation starts with your commitment to living true to who you are at your essence. Being a catalyst for transformation in your relationships calls for (a) a commitment to being an empowering influence, and (b) being authentically curious vs. being judgmental. Learn to ask questions, like "What's important to you about that?" Help the other person access their deeper want, and raise their self-awareness of what is driving their choices or behavior.

Calling Forth Greatness Inquiry: How am I contributing to profound, long-lasting positive change for myself and others?

Reflect on this Calling Forth Greatness Inquiry in your journal for a day or a week. Notice what shows up. Journal your learning here:

There can be no more important task in our life than to get in touch with our own inner self, the source of all Being. The deepest self within each of us is the Self of the whole universe, and it's also the source of all healing and transformation.

~Deepak Chopra, MD

Wisdom SIX Call Forth Greatness

To be what we are and become what we're capable of becoming is the meaning of this world.
~Robert Louis Stevenson

Coaches know the impact of reflecting their client's greatness, so clients can raise their awareness of who they are and build their capacity for living more fully from their greatness.

Coaches create the environment necessary for clients to explore, expand, and deepen their connection to their essential self, resulting in greater belief, faith, trust, and love for themselves.

In these profoundly changing times, there is a definite shift in society toward people understanding that to make lasting changes to our outer reality we need to change our inner state of being. The first step is to become aware of what our inner reality is—an innately magnificent nature.

Our ability to see the greatness in our partners, family, friends, colleagues, community, and the world is only as effective as our ability to see the greatness in ourselves. Relating to ourselves and others from an open, heartfelt space allows us to access the natural wisdom and greatness inherent within, giving rise to the ultimate in authentic living with greater focus, clarity, honesty, integrity, and balance.

The greatest discovery of our generation is the discovery that human beings, by changing the inner attitudes of their minds, can change the outer aspects of their lives.
~William James

If you want more joy, satisfaction, fulfillment, peace, ease, or freedom in your life, then the place to start is to claim your inner wisdom and natural greatness. You are a bright light at the natural state of your true self. Thinking anything less is a diminishment of your essential nature.

At first, it may be uncomfortable for you to speak of yourself in terms of greatness. Most of us were told by our elders not to brag or boast. Many people are uncomfortable saying "I have greatness within me." This is not bragging or boasting. This is about claiming the truth — your essential truth.

Coaches develop the skill of listening deeply for their client's greatness, especially , noticing the positive qualities of their character that they are expressing or the values they are honoring. Coaches reflect those qualities using a skill called "acknowledgment." For example, the coach might say to the client, "I noticed the courage you demonstrated when you faced that challenge." Or, "I see you honoring your value of family in that choice you made."

An acknowledgment is different than a compliment. A compliment is about you. It's not about the other person. For example, "I like your shirt." Or, "That's a beautiful dress." Compliments have a positive impact. Acknowledgments go deeper and shine a light on the essence of the other person. This is a powerful way to let the other person experience being seen or heard as their greatness.

Practice noticing qualities of how people are being. For example: courageous, bold, brave, creative, thoughtful, innovative, heroic, caring, loving, passionate, etc. Offer your reflections and watch them rise to see and own their own greatness.

The grain of wheat has died to its small self,
so it can be released to its greatness.
~Anonymous

Calling Forth Greatness Inquiry: How fully am I living into my greatness and calling forth the greatness in others?

Reflect on this Calling Forth Greatness Inquiry in your journal for a day or a week. Notice what shows up. Journal your learning here:

____

____

____

____

____

____

____

____

What lies behind us and what lies before us are tiny matters compared to what lies within us.
~Ralph Waldo Emerson

Wisdom SEVEN Hold them BIG

You have powers you never dreamed of. You can do things you never thought you could do. There are no limitations in what you can do except the limitations of your own mind.
~Darwin P. Kingsley

A fundamental principle of the coaching paradigm is based on the belief that *everyone is creative, capable, and resourceful.* Coaches learn there is no need for "fixing." People are not projects. When we are treated as such, we don't typically respond well, do we? We feel diminished, small, and incapable of making our own choices and decisions.

People will naturally raise their self-confidence and self-esteem when held in trust, respect and unconditional regard.

Greater self-confidence leads to increased self-awareness, performance, and fulfillment. Human psychology indicates that when awareness is raised from the unconscious level to the conscious level, people access more of their authentic power and will begin making better choices. They can then change their limiting perspectives, beliefs, and habits and begin developing more empowering perspectives, behaviors, and practices.

Here are some of the ways coaches hold their clients "BIG":

- **Ask vs. Tell** – Ask a curious question that invites or challenges the client to look deeper within to discover their personal truth, access core strengths, or learn something about themselves, instead of offering opinions, advice, or suggestions. Whether the input is solicited or unsolicited, this sends a subtle message that the client is not seen as creative, capable, or resourceful.

- **Make a Powerful Request** – Based on what the client has indicated they want, make a request that challenges the client to stretch, so they set the bar high for themselves, higher than they would otherwise set for themselves.

- **Support Accountability** – Coaches don't hold their clients accountable. They support clients in holding themselves accountable, so they can successfully learn, grow, build on their own strengths, and develop new capacities.

- **Hold the Silence** – Resist the temptation to fill the silence, so the person can hear themselves think. Allow any discomfort. Coaches get out of the way and let the client "do their own heavy lifting."

- **Suspend Judgment** – Without judgment present, fear is minimized. In the absence of fear, creativity, joy, and passion can emerge.

It can be a transformative experience for others when we simply pause instead of immediately filling up space. And by holding others BIG, we create a sacred space for their innate wisdom, willingness to risk, and courage to emerge.

At the level of Courage, an attainment of true power occurs; therefore, it's also the level of empowerment. This is the zone of exploration, accomplishment, fortitude, and determination. At the lower levels, the world is seen as hopeless, sad, frightening, or frustrating; but at the level of Courage, life is seen to be exciting, challenging, and stimulating.
~David R. Hawkins, PhD

The word courage comes from the Middle English and Old French word corage, meaning "heart." It is a human behavior that is admirable and often selfless – the stuff of epics, legends, and heroism. Courage comes from commitment, care and love. According to Gus Lee, author of *Courage, the Backbone of Leadership*, "Courage is a deep-seated, fundamental human competence that leverages our other abilities. It invokes within us our absolute best selves. The tremendous results purchased by courageous behaviors can't be replaced."

I am always, always, *always* moved to tears in the presence of Olympic athletes and my own clients – actually, anyone who is striving to perform their personal best. I am inspired by the heroism of the human spirit that risks and stretches beyond perceived limitations. Whether they "win" or they "lose," they gain in their confidence, self-esteem, and learning. And that's a winner winning.

This is the hero's journey, requiring that we leave our comfort zone to achieve our goal. We have the opportunity of playing a role in supporting others on their grand journey and we have the privilege of witnessing their greatness along the way. The key is calling forth our own greatness and knowing that we can change the world only by changing ourselves.

Calling Forth Greatness Inquiry: How will I hold myself and others BIG?

Reflect on this Calling Forth Greatness Inquiry in your journal for a day or a week. Notice what shows up. Journal your learning here:

We all have the extraordinary coded within us
Waiting to be released.
~Jean Houston

Michelle Miranda - Thank you, Michelle, for the inspiration to write this book. I will never forget the day you said to me, "Fran, you are THE ONE to write the book about the spirituality of coaching." Your words ignited my spirit. By the end of that same day, I had already outlined the contents of this book.

My Author Support Group: Ron Rael, Toolie Gardner, and Emiko Hori – Thank you for your ongoing support, honest feedback, personal championing, and creative and insightful contributions to my writing and publishing projects, including this one.

Friends and Colleagues: Gloria Knapp, Madi Navon, Gloria Maxx, Sandra Jones, MJ Schwader, Annie Gelfand, and all my coaching students, clients, and coaches over the years, who have been my inspiration and teachers on my learning journey.

Below, you will read my bio, but what I really want to share with you is my passion for bringing the empowerment philosophy and principles of coaching into everyday living. My vision is a world where the coaching approach is woven into our fabric of living.

Fran Fisher is a Master Certified Coach (MCC), visionary leader, international speaker, and published author. She specializes in providing training, coaching and mentoring for beginning as well as seasoned coaches, and coaching services for leaders who are affecting positive and meaningful influence in their organization, personal life, and the world.

Recipient of The Lifetime Achievement Award 2012 by the ICF Chapter Washington State, Fran is recognized internationally as one of the pioneers and champions for coaching. She served as a founding International Coach Federation, ICF, Executive Board member, and co-chair of the Ethics and Standards Committee, responsible for developing the Credentialing Programs for aspiring coaches and training schools. Fran was the first Executive Director of the Association for Coach Training Organizations, ACTO. She has been serving as an ICF Credentialing Assessor since 1998.

Fran's passion is helping people liberate their authentic power and manifest their highest visions. She specializes in facilitating a transformational approach for blending the art of visioning with the structure of strategic planning and intuitive listening to empower her clients for greater success and fulfillment.

In 1991, Fran founded the Living Your Vision® (LYV) process for empowering individuals in transforming their visions into reality. In 1997, Fran founded the Academy for Coach Training, one of the first International Coach Federation (ICF) accredited schools. In 2006, she sold the ACT and LYV businesses and their associated trademarks to I & AM, LLC dba INVITEchange.

Fran is the author of the following books:

- *Violet's Vision*
  www.violetsvision.com

- *The Illusion of Hopelessness*
  www.illusionofhopelessness.com

- *Calling Forth Greatness*
  https://www.facebook.com/fran.fisher.mcc

- Co-author: *Empowerment Selling*
  www.empowermentselling.com

- Contributing author:
  NO Winner Ever Got There Without a Coach. Fran's chapter is titled: Living True to Your Essence.

Fran lives in Bellevue, Washington, USA. In her leisure time, she enjoys ballroom dancing, long walks on ocean beaches, and hiking Pacific Northwest trails. She recently accomplished her 20-year bucket-list goal of walking the path of the Camino de Santiago pilgrimage.

Please feel free to connect with Fran!

www.franfishercoach.com
fran@franfishercoach.com
1+425-401-1374

LinkedIn: Fran Fisher
Facebook: Fran Fisher Coach
Facebook Page:
CallingForthGreatnessBOOK

For more information about Fran's coaching products and services, go to www.franfishercoach.com

- Books
- Blogs
- Free Teleclasses
- Coaching for individuals, executives, business owners, coaches
- Mentoring for coaches: 1:1 or small groups
- My Portable Mentor – downloadable audio series and materials for coaches

Made in United States
North Haven, CT
25 August 2024